Wildlife
Making a Comeback
How Humans Are Helping

by Judith E. Rinard

Famous symbol, the bald eagle stands for the United States of America. Chosen as the national bird in 1782, it appears on U. S. coins and on the nation's great seal. Yet, few Americans have seen a bald eagle in the wild. By the 1960s, the species was dying out from habitat loss, illegal hunting, and pesticide poisoning. Now, it is making a comeback.

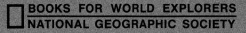 BOOKS FOR WORLD EXPLORERS
NATIONAL GEOGRAPHIC SOCIETY

Contents

COVER: *Like a lion's mane, red-gold fur frames the face of a golden lion tamarin. This squirrel-size monkey lives at the National Zoological Park's breeding center, near Front Royal, Virginia. Its habitat is the Atlantic coastal forest in Brazil, which has been almost completely cut down. Now, golden lion tamarins are endangered. A worldwide effort to save them involves breeding the animals in zoos and later placing them in a forest reserve, an area set aside for wildlife, in Brazil.*

NATIONAL GEOGRAPHIC PHOTOGRAPHER JAMES L. AMOS

Four cheetah cubs play near their mother on the Serengeti Plain, in Africa. Fastest of all land animals, cheetahs can sprint more than 70 miles an hour (113 km/h).* Yet today, they may be running out of time in a race against extinction. Illegally hunted for their fur and driven from their habitat by farmers, cheetahs may be extinct by the end of this century unless humans help them survive.

MITSUAKI IWAGO

*Metric figures in this book have been rounded off.

Copyright © 1987 National Geographic Society
Library of Congress CIP data: page 103

North America

South America

Wildlife Around the World

All over the world, thousands of species of plants and animals are becoming extinct—disappearing forever. Loss of habitat, overhunting, and pollution are three of the major causes of extinctions.

As earth's human population grows, people put more and more pressure on wild things, both plant and animal. At the same time, many people all over the world are working to save species. The good news is that some species have made comebacks. For many others, the outcome is still uncertain. What people do today and tomorrow will make a difference in the lives of various kinds of creatures.

WILDLIFE: *Making a Comeback* includes many endangered and threatened species and a number of those making successful comebacks. The map on these pages is not a range map. It simply locates in the wild the creatures shown in this book. The true size of each one is not indicated, and each may live in more than the one location given here. Some of the animals are still endangered but are making comebacks. Others are now

Europe

Asia

Africa

Australia

declining and can make comebacks only with continued help from humans.

North America—United States: **(1)** bald eagle, **(2)** grizzly bear, **(3)** northern sea lion, **(4)** desert tortoise, **(5)** gray whale, **(6)** northern elephant seal, **(7)** brown pelican, **(8)** dusky seaside sparrow (This bird became extinct during the preparation of the book.), **(9)** manatee, **(10)** great gray owl, **(11)** eastern bluebird, **(12)** peregrine falcon, **(13)** bison, **(14)** pronghorn, **(15)** trumpeter swan, **(16)** whooping crane, **(17)** mountain lion. Canada: **(18)** polar bear, **(19)** white-tailed deer, **(20)** Atlantic salmon, **(21)** gray wolf. **South America**—Brazil: **(22)** caiman, **(23)** golden lion tamarin. Ecuador, Galápagos Islands: **(24)** Galápagos tortoise. Peru: **(25)** vicuña. **Africa**—Kenya: **(26)** white rhinoceros. Namibia: **(27)** African elephant. Gabon: **(28)** lowland gorilla. Tanzania: **(29)** black rhinoceros, **(30)** cheetah. Madagascar: **(31)** rosy periwinkle (not endangered). **Asia**—India: **(32)** Bengal tiger, **(33)** gaur calf. China: **(34)** Chinese alligator, **(35)** snow leopard. Mongolia: **(36)** Przewalski's horse. Sri Lanka: **(37)** rusty spotted cat. Oman: **(38)** Arabian oryx. Indonesia: **(39)** Bali mynah. **Australia**— **(40)** flying fox, **(41)** ring-tailed rock wallaby, **(42)** Lord Howe Island wood hen. New Zealand: **(43)** red deer (not endangered). LOIS SLOAN

1
Helping Vanishing Wildlife

The mountain lion had left her two kittens hidden in a cave high in the canyon wall. As she hunted for food, she suddenly caught the scent of people and dogs. Before the hunters saw her, the big cat swiftly climbed the rocks of the canyon, moving silently and keeping out of sight of her enemies. When the mountain lion was certain that she had not been followed, she returned to her kittens and curled her warm body around them. Tomorrow, she would take them with her and go deeper into the wilderness, far away from the humans who hunted with dogs and guns.

Once, the mountain lion's range covered most of North, Central, and South America. This big cat is known by many names, including cougar, panther, and puma. Some Indians worshiped the cat. "Puma" (PYOO-muh or POO-muh) comes from the language of the Inca Indians of Peru. It meant "courage and power."

Early settlers of the United States hunted mountain lions because they sometimes killed livestock. For years, ranchers made an effort to wipe them out. By 1960, the big cats had nearly disappeared from

Powerful hunter, a mountain lion peers from a snowy ledge. Mountain lions once lived in most of North, Central, and South America. As ranchers shot them to protect livestock, the cats rapidly disappeared. Rewards called bounties were paid for their hides. By 1960, only a few thousand of these big cats were left in the United States, mostly in the mountainous West. Now that hunting laws protect mountain lions, they are making a comeback.

DANIEL J. COX

the eastern United States. In the West, they were found only in remote areas where humans seldom lived or hunted. So few were left that scientists feared mountain lions might die out.

In 1964, Dr. Maurice Hornocker, a biologist, began to track and study mountain lions in the wilderness of Idaho in an effort to save them. He learned that they are shy and solitary—and seldom a threat to livestock. He also learned that mountain lions play a beneficial role in nature. They tend to kill old, sick, or weak members of deer herds. This helps keep the herd from outgrowing its food supply.

As a result of this research, hunting laws were changed to protect mountain lions. Now, they are making a comeback in the West. "They're doing very well," says Hornocker. "Protection by people can help animals like these."

Many animals that once nearly died out have been saved with the help of people. Another example is the California gray whale. In the 19th century, whalers killed so many of these animals for blubber to make oil that the gray whale almost disappeared. In the 1940s, several nations agreed to stop the hunting of this ocean mammal. With international protection, gray whales greatly increased in number.

Would you like to meet a gray whale face to face? Every year, thousands of people do. They travel on excursion boats to warm waters off Baja California, part of Mexico. There, gray whales breed and have their young. These areas have been set aside by the Mexican government as whale sanctuaries. Excursion boats must have permits to visit them. "Visiting the whales is very exciting," says Dale Sydenstricker, of San Diego, California, who works for an excursion boat company. "The whales bring their young to see us. The whale mothers remind me of human mothers who take their babies to the zoo! The whales come right up to the boat and

"Hi!" a curious gray whale seems to say as it swims up to be petted by whale watchers. Here, in warm waters off Baja California, in Mexico, the whales come each year to mate and to give birth. In the 19th century, gray whales were nearly wiped out by whalers who killed them for blubber to make oil. Now, they are protected by law. The 80,000-pound (36,288-kg) giants seem to like people. "They're so friendly and gentle—like great big dogs," says one observer. "Their skin feels like soft rubber."

The great auk, a large penguin-like bird, was hunted to extinction by humans. By the 1830s, historians described the auk as being as "dead as a dodo," another extinct bird. Great auks nested on islands of the North Atlantic Ocean. Because they could not fly, the birds were easy prey for sailors, who killed thousands of them for food. In 1844, the last two great auks in the world were killed to be stuffed for a wealthy man's collection.

THE BETTMANN ARCHIVE

let people pet them. They are friendly and curious."

Once, the earth was amazingly rich in wildlife. People hunted without thinking of the future, for the supply of animals seemed unlimited. Today, however, we know that when too many animals of one species, or kind, are killed, that species will die out. When the last member of a species dies, the species becomes extinct. "Extinct" means "no longer living or found on earth." Once an animal is extinct, it is gone forever. There is no way of getting it back.

Extinction is a natural process that has always occurred on earth. For example, millions of years ago, the dinosaurs became extinct. Many scientists believe they died out because they could not adapt, or adjust, to changes in the earth and its climate. In just the last three centuries, however, *thousands* of plant and animal species have become extinct. Most of those extinctions occurred not because of natural changes on earth, but because of the activities of humans. Today, more species are in danger of extinction.

People have killed huge numbers of animals for their fur, feathers, hides, horns, teeth, blubber, or other body parts. Overhunting has caused the extinction of some species. In this century, however, the greatest cause of extinction has been the destruction of habitats—the places where animals and plants live. People have used the land to build farms, houses, factories, and highways. People have also destroyed habitats by polluting them with factory wastes and chemical poisons.

Without habitats, most animals and plants cannot survive. Read more about habitats on pages 12 and 13.

Today, humans are worried about the large number and the rapid rate of extinctions—a wave unlike anything in the earth's history. To prevent extinctions, many people, especially conservationists, are working to save wildlife. "To conserve" means "to save, to protect, or to use wisely." Conservationists try to protect both plants and animals from extinction, and to help those that are nearly extinct make comebacks.

One way people can help is by passing laws to stop the killing or collecting of endangered species (those in danger of extinction). An example of such a law is the United States Endangered Species Act of 1973.

Another way to protect wildlife is by setting aside areas of wild habitat as parks and wildlife refuges and preserves. There are more than 3,500 such protected areas in the world today. In those areas, people are forbidden to harm or disturb any living thing.

A third way to help wildlife is by studying species of plants and animals in *(Continued on page 15)*

Orange Band, a dusky seaside sparrow, was the last of his species. These small birds lived in the marshes of eastern Florida. In the 1950s, there were thousands of them. Then the marshes were sprayed with pesticides and drained to build a highway. By 1980, only five dusky seaside sparrows remained. On June 16, 1987, during the preparation of this book, Orange Band died of old age. "It's sad to say good-bye to the last creature of its kind on earth," says Charles Cook, curator of the Discovery Island Zoological Park at the Walt Disney World Resort, in Orlando, where the sparrow lived. "People feel a great loss when a species disappears from the earth."

Worlds of Wildlife

From the highest mountains to the deepest oceans, earth with its many climates provides a great variety of homes for plants and animals. These homes are called habitats. Here, you see various habitats and some of the plants and animals that live in them. Over millions of years, all of these creatures have become adapted, or suited, to their own special homes. Unlike people, most of them cannot easily adjust to different habitats.

If you look closely at some of the animals here, you will see how their bodies are suited to living where they do. For example, the polar bear has a thick fur coat to help keep it warm in the icy north. It could not survive in a hot rain forest or in a hot desert. The orangutan and the cactus are well adapted

to heat; they could not live in a land of ice and snow.

Habitats provide animals with food, water, shelter, and places to have their young. People once believed that animals in danger of extinction could be saved by simply protecting them from hunting. Today, however, experts say we must also protect the animals' living space. Without their habitats, animals will die out even if they are not hunted.

All the animals on these pages have suffered from changes in their habitats. Their homes have been overgrazed; paved for roads; cleared for timber or to build community resorts and farms; and polluted by oil spills, pesticides, and factory wastes. For all these animals, the future will depend on whether people can preserve what remains of their habitats.

LOIS SLOAN

Homes of Animals and Plants

1 **Tropical rain forest**—Orangutan
2 **Coral reef**—Tropical fish
3 **Ocean**—Gray whale
4 **River**—Atlantic salmon
5 **Swamp**—Water frog
6 **Marsh**—American alligator
7 **Desert**—Cactus
8 **Tundra**—Lemming
9 **Arctic**—Polar bear
10 **Evergreen forest**—Wild turkey
11 **Dry plain**—Coyote
12 **Prairie**—Bison
13 **Mountain ridge**—Bighorn sheep
14 **Seasonal forest**—Bald eagle
15 **African grassland**—Zebra

(Continued from page 10) their natural habitats. With more knowledge of how creatures live in the wild, people can better protect them.

Finally, when species can no longer survive in their habitats, experts can keep captive individuals and try to breed them. Some can then be released into protected wild areas. Today, many zoos have such programs.

Zoos also help educate people about endangered wildlife and why it needs to be protected. Why *should* people care if wildlife species become extinct? There are many reasons.

First, wild animals and plants add beauty and wonder to the world. Imagine how camping would be without trees, flowers, fish, birds, butterflies, or deer. If all the earth's wild cats or great whales had died out, nobody could see or touch one today. There would be only pictures of these animals. No photograph or film can ever replace a living animal or the human experience of seeing it alive.

Wild animals and plants give humans many things necessary to their existence. Fish, for example, provide food for much of the world. Wild relatives of domestic food plants—for example, corn or strawberries—are crossbred with crop varieties to make them resistant to disease. Plants also provide important medicines. About a fourth of all prescription drugs contain chemicals found in wild plants.

Finally, all living things on earth interact with one another. If a key species is destroyed, its loss may trigger the loss of other species. To find out more about key species, read about flying foxes on pages 18–21.

Humans can do much to help endangered wildlife today. A good example (Continued on page 23)

Angel, a cheetah "goodwill ambassador" from the Cincinnati Zoo, visits a classroom in Withamsville, Ohio. Zoo educator Cathryn Hilker holds Angel, as co-worker Cathy Tompson paints cheetah face marks on Amy Connelly, 13. The students are learning about endangered animals. The face marks on the cheetah help it survive in its home in Africa by possibly absorbing sunlight and cutting down glare. "Angel was shy and pretty," says Amy, who had never been so close to a cheetah before. "We even heard her purr! I'm angry that some people hunt and kill cheetahs for their fur."

A girl of Madagascar, an island off the southeast coast of Africa, holds a life-saving plant of the tropical forest—the rosy periwinkle (below). If this species had become extinct just 20 years ago, scientists would never have known that the rosy periwinkle contains chemicals for treating cancer. Today, a drug made from this plant helps save the lives of people with leukemia, a form of cancer.

FRANS LANTING

In a rain forest of Colombia, a country in South America, scientist Dr. Alwyn Gentry (right) examines an unknown species of plant he found. Experts believe the world's rain forests are a treasury of natural-healing and disease-fighting drugs. The forests are being destroyed so quickly, however, that many of the precious plants may become extinct before they can be discovered.

NATIONAL GEOGRAPHIC PHOTOGRAPHER JAMES P. BLAIR

Flying Foxes: Keystone Species

Hanging from a branch, a furry bat in Australia sips nectar from a blossom. As it does, the bat gets a meal—and it helps the tree and many creatures that live in the tree survive.

This bat is called a flying fox because of its fox-like snout and ears. By spreading pollen from blossom to blossom as it feeds, the bat pollinates the tree, enabling it to reproduce.

Without bats, this kind of tree might not survive, because it could not produce fertile seeds. Then, many other animals that depend on the tree for food and shelter might die, too.

MERLIN D. TUTTLE, BAT CONSERVATION INTERNATIONAL

lying foxes live in Asia, Africa, and Australia, as well as on islands of the Pacific Ocean. Scientists call some species of these bats "keystone species." The central—or key—stone in an arch supports all the other stones. Similarly, the activities of some bats support whole communities of living things—both animals and plants. Without certain bats, many of those living things might not survive.

Dr. Merlin Tuttle, a biologist and a bat expert, says, "In the tropics, some trees have flowers that open only at night. As bats visit the blossoms to sip nectar, they carry pollen from one flower to another. In this way, they pollinate the trees, enabling them to bear fruit with fertile seeds. The night-blooming trees depend on the bats, and many animals depend on the trees. Destruction of bats could cause a chain reaction of extinctions."

Besides pollination, bats serve another useful function. When they eat fruits, such as mangoes,

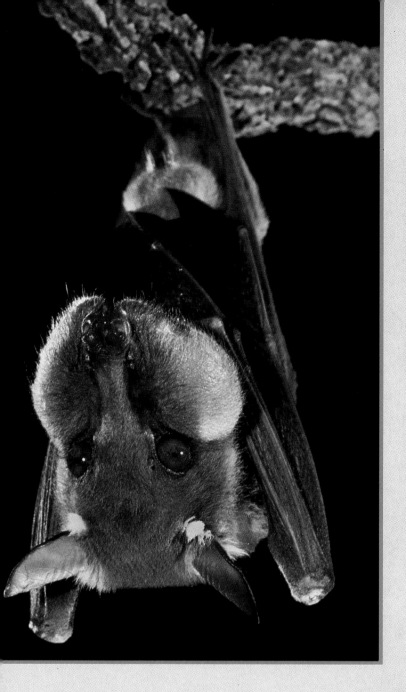

MERLIN D. TUTTLE, BAT CONSERVATION INTERNATIONAL (ALL)

Going, going, gone! A bat called a flying fox bites off a ripe fig, takes it into its mouth, chews it, then swallows it and licks its lips. As the bat flies, it will deposit fig seeds in its droppings. Some of the seeds may sprout and grow into trees. In this way, bats help trees multiply, providing more food for other animals, such as parrots and monkeys.

dates, and figs and then fly away, they scatter fruit seeds in their droppings. Some of the seeds sprout and grow into new trees, which replace trees that have died or been cut down.

Yet, in spite of the good they do, bats are in danger of becoming extinct. People shoot them as pests, for food, or simply out of fear. "The biggest threat to all bats today," says Tuttle, "is misunderstanding. Bats are night creatures and not easily seen; people fear them."

How can bats be saved? Tuttle believes that education is the way. He heads a group called Bat Conservation International, which studies bats and spreads knowledge about them. Greater human understanding may prevent bat extinction.

"We must learn to protect important animals like bats," says Tuttle, "or we endanger the environment we all must share."

(Continued from page 15) of an animal comeback is the elephant seal, one of the largest seals. Males may weigh up to 6,000 pounds (2,722 kg). The animals get their name from the huge nose of the adult male.

Northern elephant seals once came ashore to breed and to give birth to young on many beaches of Mexico and California. In the 19th century, they were killed for their blubber to make oil. By 1900, the species was nearly extinct. Fewer than a hundred animals were left. The Mexican government began to protect the seals by outlawing seal hunting. Then, in 1972, the United States passed the Marine Mammal Protection Act. It makes killing marine mammals, including the elephant seal, illegal without special permission.

Today, large numbers of elephant seals come each year to breeding grounds on Año Nuevo Island and nearby mainland California. These areas are now included in the Año Nuevo State Reserve, a protected wildlife habitat and park.

"Our main job here is to protect the animals and their habitat," says Gary Strachan, the supervising park ranger at Año Nuevo. "To do it, you have to care about the animals. It's exciting that so many kids come here and get interested in the work we do," Strachan continues.

In the next chapters, you'll discover more about endangered animals and how people are helping them.

Elephant seal pups (left) huddle together at Año Nuevo State Reserve in California. Here, on protected beaches, thousands of northern elephant seals come ashore each year to mate and to have their young.

FRANS LANTING (BOTH)

Researchers attach a tag to the fin of an elephant seal pup (above). The tag, which does not hurt the seal, will help scientists identify it and keep track of it.

Two male elephant seals snort and bellow in a fierce battle for mates at Año Nuevo State Reserve. Thousands of visitors come each year to the reserve, one of the few places in the world where the public can watch these animals in their natural habitat. On guided tours, visitors also see mother seals and pups. To avoid disturbing the animals, people must observe certain rules and approach no closer than 20 feet (6 m).

KENNAN WARD ©

2 Saving Habitats

If you visited a tropical rain forest, you would find a lush, green world alive with plants and animals. Colorful parrots and bright butterflies sail among the sunlit treetops. Farther down, monkeys chatter and swing through the branches, and tiny birds of rainbow colors dart among the leaves and flowers. On the shadowy forest floor, spotted cats stalk prey; giant snakes slither; insects hop and swarm.

Tropical rain forests are the richest habitats for wildlife of all the earth's lands. They are found in the hot, humid tropics, especially in Central and South America, in Africa, and in Asia. Scientists estimate that 50 percent or more of all the species of plants and animals on earth live in these forests. Yet the forests are being destroyed at an alarming rate.

People sell the trees for timber or cut them for firewood. Then they use the land for crops and cattle, cities and mines. As the forests are cut, hundreds of species of plants and animals disappear each year. If the forests are not saved, much of earth's wildlife will be lost.

The loss of wildlife habitats is not a problem just in

A logger's chain saw rips through a tree in a tropical rain forest in Papua New Guinea, a nation north of Australia. This tree, the home of many animals, will probably be ground into tiny chips for manufacturing cardboard. Tropical rain forests provide homes for more than half of all earth's species of plants and animals. Yet, people are rapidly destroying forests for firewood, for charcoal, for timber, and for land to raise crops and cattle. Loss of habitat is the biggest threat to all wildlife today.

NATIONAL GEOGRAPHIC PHOTOGRAPHER JAMES P. BLAIR

tropical countries. It is a problem all over the world. In North America, forests provide homes for owls, woodpeckers, squirrels, deer, beavers, snakes, bears, wolves, and other animals. Many of the forests that once covered the continent were cut down to make room for cities and farms. Other trees are still being cut for lumber to build homes and for pulp to make paper.

In the United States and Canada, government agencies and private companies manage most forestlands. Each year, they allow more areas of forest to be cut. Often, forests are replanted with seedlings. Some trees are never cut, but are preserved as homes for wildlife.

The spotted owl, for example, prefers to build its nest in old trees. It looks for tree trunks softened by decay. When limbs fall off old trees, any holes that remain make ideal nesting places. The U. S. Forest Service is trying to keep spotted owls from becoming endangered

RICH FRISHMAN (ABOVE)

Boy Scouts bring new life to a forest cut by loggers in Washington State. Zach Mayer, at left, and David Andrews, both 10 and from Ridgefield, plant fir seedlings on a snowy spring day. "Afterward, we were cold and tired, but happy," says Zach. "Many animals need the trees for homes, so we were glad to help."

In a clear-cut section of an Idaho forest, a great gray owl perches on a dead tree. Owls hunt by first listening for the sounds of small animals on the ground. Then they swoop down on their prey. In many areas, logging destroys most of their listening posts, making it harder for the owls to find food. Some kinds of owls—the spotted owl, for example— are threatened because of loss of habitat.

MICHAEL S. QUINTON (RIGHT)

*Gently touching and nuzzling each other, manatees swim
in the Crystal River, a sanctuary in Florida. Manatees are
mammals, not fish. They must surface regularly to
breathe. Because of human invasion of their habitat,
they are now in danger of becoming extinct.*

in Washington State. "First, we must find the owls," says Joan Kittrell, of the Forest Service. "We go out at night and hoot. When the owls answer, we catch them in traps set with mice." After attaching radio transmitters to the trapped owls, biologists release them and track them to learn where they live. Then that part of the forest—important to the owls—is saved.

The Forest Service cooperates with Boy Scouts and Girl Scouts eager to help replant clear-cut areas. Clear-cutting is the practice of cutting *all* the trees in an area. Jaa Schue, 17, and his brother, Red, 11, of Vancouver, Washington, took part in this program for several years.

"When I first went there, the clear-cut area was lifeless," says Jaa. "Our troop planted a hundred seedlings in an hour. A year later when I returned, I was amazed at how the trees had grown. I'm glad, because I love wildlife. Animals need trees for food, homes, and cover."

Experts agree, however, that replanting does not replace lost forests. A forest of new trees cannot support the variety of wildlife found in an old forest.

The activities of humans also threaten the habitats of water animals. In the coastal waters of the southeastern United States and in the Caribbean Sea live gentle mammals called manatees. According to Dr. Jesse White, a marine mammal veterinarian with the Florida Department of Natural Resources, many manatees die from motorboat injuries. As the slow-moving animals come to the surface to breathe, the spinning propellers of speedboats may cut deeply into their flesh. White has rescued many manatees. He has also helped them breed in captivity.

Now, in 1987, only about 1,200 manatees are left in U. S. waters. Since these animals are endangered, federal and state laws protect them. Florida has established 21 official manatee sanctuaries, or places of safety.

All over the world, governments and private conservation groups are taking steps to protect wildlife habitats. For example, an international conservation group called Ducks Unlimited helped save Cranberry Marsh, in the Canadian province of British Columbia, as a bird refuge. Years ago, this marsh was a natural breeding ground for ducks and geese. Gradually, however, the plants took over, and the marsh no longer had enough open water where birds could land and find food.

In the late 1970s, Ducks Unlimited surveyed the area. By 1981, the group had built a system of water channels around islands in the marsh. "This system makes a perfect breeding site for ducks and geese," says the marsh manager, Murray Clark. "The islands provide safe nesting places away from predators, and the waterways

Signs like this metal outline of two manatees warn boaters to slow down and to watch for the animals in certain Florida waterways. Manatees move slowly and cannot get out of the way of speeding motorboats. Many have been cut or killed by spinning boat propellers. To protect the animals, Florida has established 21 sanctuaries for manatees. During certain times of year, boaters in those areas must reduce their speed. In some sanctuaries, boating is strictly forbidden. Anyone who intentionally harms a manatee may have to pay a large fine and possibly even go to jail.

supply plenty of plants and animals for the birds to eat.'' Cranberry Marsh now attracts people, too, who come to watch and enjoy the birds.

All over the world, nations have set aside wildlife habitats as refuges and parks. Conservationists hope that countries with tropical rain forests will protect parts of these habitats before they are all destroyed. For example, scientists of the World Wildlife Fund (WWF), an international conservation group, are studying the rain forest of the Amazon in Brazil. Their goal is to learn how much of it needs to be saved to keep the animals and plants found there from becoming extinct.

To do their research, the WWF scientists cooperated with Brazil's National Institute for Amazon Research, as well as with ranchers who are cutting the trees to make room for raising cattle. The researchers arranged for loggers to leave about 20 (Continued on page 37)

A watery maze? No. This is a breeding and nesting ground for wild ducks and geese. In 1981, Ducks Unlimited, an international conservation group, decided to improve this Canadian site. It is Cranberry Marsh, in British Columbia. The marsh had become so overgrown with plants that few water birds could use it. Engineers built a system of waterways around nesting islands and made an ideal habitat. Now the marsh attracts flocks of mallards, teal, Canada geese, and many other birds.

DAVID CARMACK

Justin Tavares, 15, of Washington, D. C., works as a junior zoo keeper at the National Zoological Park. "My favorite part of the job is feeding dry cat food to the ducks," says Justin. "They swim right up when they see me." Wood ducks often join Justin's feeding parties. Once rare due to overhunting and loss of habitat, wood ducks are now plentiful because of protective laws.

GEORG GERSTER

33

In Etosha National Park, elephants wander onto a road in Namibia, a country in southwestern Africa. Etosha is one of the largest of Africa's wildlife reserves. On its 8,600 square miles (22,272 km²) live herds of zebras, giraffes, antelope, and elephants, as well as lions and cheetahs. Tourists from all over the world come to see the wildlife. They drive around the park on special roads. The money the visitors pay in entry fees helps support the reserve, which in turn protects the animals.

JIM BRANDENBURG

(Continued from page 33)   islands of forest for them to study. Sizes varied from 2½ acres to 2,500 acres.

The scientists first took a census, or count, of the wildlife in the forest before the cutting began. They studied birds, monkeys, insects, and other animals, as well as trees and smaller plants. They camped in the forest, sleeping in hammocks under a plastic roof.

Victor Bullen and Marie Uehling, both of Washington, D. C., worked on this rain forest project in Brazil. Bullen is a wildland management expert. Uehling is a botanist, or plant expert.

"It was hard work," says Bullen. "I was on a bird census team. We got up at 4:30 every morning to set large nets called mist nets. The mesh is so fine the birds don't see the nets. They are not harmed when they fly into them. By 6:30, we began checking for birds. Using metal rings, we banded one leg of each bird we caught. After taking notes on the birds, we released them. By afternoon, we were exhausted and dripping with sweat. We bathed in a stream, had supper, and went to bed. Nets around our hammocks protected us from the insects."

After the forest was cut and cleared by burning, the researchers returned. "It was a shock," says Uehling. "I could hardly believe that the forest where we had awakened each morning to the sound of monkeys now looked like Hiroshima after the atomic bombing."

Later, when the scientists studied the islands of forest left standing, they found that most were far too small to support the original variety of wildlife. Many animals had disappeared or died because they could not find food or could not survive in cramped conditions.

"What we have found so far," says Bullen, "is strong evidence for the need to set aside large parcels of the rain forest as parkland. Only in that way will this habitat and its wildlife be able to survive."

Cutting down a forest is a *direct* way of destroying

In a laboratory, botanist Marie Uehling studies tree cuttings collected from the rain forest before logging began. "We've collected more than 60,000 so far," she says, "many unknown to science. We were amazed at the variety of trees. Workers went high into the treetops to gather leaves, flowers, and fruits. Studying them will help us learn a lot about the life of the rain forest."

Researchers take a count of the birds in an area of forest to be left uncut. Jan Smith attaches a leg band to a blue-crowned motmot, as Steve Snyder holds another bird. Opal Dakin notes the kinds of birds netted and banded here—a total of 175 species. When the surrounding forest was cut, most species gradually disappeared.

In a clear-cut area near Manaus, Brazil, a patch of tropical rain forest (left) is a tiny island of life. The forest is being cleared to raise cattle. Researchers from the World Wildlife Fund, along with Brazilian scientists, are studying forest plots of varying sizes before and after logging takes place. They want to find out what happens to plants and animals when parts of the forest are cut and how big an area is needed to preserve the wildlife.

RANDALL HYMAN (ALL)

Caught in a tangle of fishing net, a sea lion has struggled ashore on a rocky island off the coast of Alaska. Every year, hundreds of seals and many sea lions become tangled in plastic nets and ropes. These materials are discarded from fishing boats and left floating in the water. As a result, many animals drown. Some, like this one, manage to swim ashore. People who spotted this sea lion rescued it by cutting off the net. "Then," says one of the rescuers, "we watched it turn away and swim free."

C. W. FOWLER

a wild habitat. This threat is easy to see. Other threats may not be visible at first, but they are just as serious. One of the greatest dangers to all habitats is pollution—including automobile exhausts, garbage, factory smoke and wastes, oil spills from ships, and pesticides.

As the world's human population increases, more and more wastes and garbage are being dumped into the seas, into rivers, and onto land. The growth of industry and manufacturing has brought ever greater pollution. Today, laws and regulations control many of these harmful wastes. Still, dangers from pollution remain. One of the most serious dangers is acid rain.

Acid rain results when harmful gases from factories, power plants, and automobiles travel high in the air—sometimes for hundreds of miles in the wind. In the clouds, the gases mix with moisture, forming acid. When the acid falls as rain or snow, it builds up in lakes and streams. There, it kills fish and other wildlife. Heavily industrialized parts of Europe as well as much of the northeastern United States and eastern Canada are polluted by acid rain.

"In Nova Scotia, acid rain has polluted numbers of rivers where salmon normally lay their eggs," says Lee Sochasky, of the Atlantic Salmon Federation, an international conservation organization. "Salmon have already disappeared from 13 of these rivers."

Today, scientists in many countries are working to stop acid rain. Most agree that the only solution is to reduce the air pollution that causes it.

Another dangerous source of pollution for wildlife is pesticides. These are powerful poisons sprayed on crops and lawns to kill harmful insects or weeds.

After World War II, a pesticide called DDT was widely used in the United States. Rain washing over the land carried the DDT into lakes and streams. A manufacturer of DDT in California *(Continued on page 44)*

A bald eagle perches on a garbage dump on the island of Adak, Alaska. Polluting the land with garbage can be deadly to wildlife. When animals feed on garbage, they may swallow poisonous chemicals or other dangerous things. "We found one eagle that had died from swallowing broken glass at a garbage dump," says Fred Zeillemaker, a wildlife refuge manager on Adak. "We now warn the public on radio and TV about this danger to animals. We ask people to bury their garbage."

Atlantic salmon swim up a river in the Canadian province of Quebec to spawn, or lay their eggs. These fish spend one to three years feeding at sea. Then they swim upstream to spawn in the same rivers in which they were hatched. Once threatened mostly by overfishing, the salmon now are also in danger from pollution. If their home rivers are polluted, the fish will not choose other streams. Instead, they will return to sea without spawning.

Trash litters a stream (above) in Nova Scotia, a province of Canada. Salmon deposit their eggs in gravel on the bottom of certain streams. The eggs need a constant supply of oxygen from clean, running water. Garbage thrown into streams, as well as dirt from road building or farm plowing, can cover the eggs. Then they die from lack of oxygen. Acid rain or snow is another major cause of pollution in salmon streams.

*Biologist Frank Gress visits a brown pelican colony
on West Anacapa Island, part of the Channel Islands
National Park, in California. In the 1960s, this species
nearly died off from eating fish containing DDT. "Now the
birds are thriving," says Gress. "Compared with only
a few hundred breeding pairs in the early 1970s, nearly
6,000 nested here in 1986."*

Taking DDT into their systems causes birds to lay eggs with abnormally thin shells. On the right (below) is a normal brown pelican egg. The other two eggs show damage from DDT. They lack the calcium needed to make shells hard. In the 1960s, many pelican eggs were so thin they broke as the birds laid them or sat on them. "DDT breaks down mostly into a compound called DDE, which stays in the environment for a very long time," says Gress. "I still occasionally find damaged eggs."

FRANS LANTING

WENDELL METZEN

A brown pelican and its chick (right) rest on Pelican Island, a sanctuary in Florida. In 1903, President Theodore Roosevelt made it the nation's first wildlife refuge. Intruders on their nesting grounds might disturb the birds, so Pelican Island is closed to the public. Brown pelicans in Florida have not suffered as much from pesticide pollution as have pelicans on the West Coast.

(Continued from page 38) dumped some of the dangerous pesticide, along with wastes, into the sea.

DDT remains in the environment indefinitely. Tiny plants and animals, both on the land and in the water, absorb the DDT into their bodies. As these small creatures are eaten by larger ones, DDT passes from one species to another.

By the 1960s, scientists had become alarmed at the numbers of large birds—such as eagles, hawks, and falcons—that were vanishing. Many birds seemed not to be reproducing.

When the scientists investigated the eggs of the birds, they found that the shells were abnormally thin. DDT had caused this thinning. The shells were so thin that most broke when the parent birds laid them or sat on them in the nests. Few hatched.

In 1972, the United States banned DDT. With this protection and with other help from humans, many of the birds—including bald eagles—have begun to make comebacks. Two real successes are the brown pelican and the peregrine falcon. Brown pelicans nest on coastal islands, especially in California and in Florida. By 1969, only a few hundred of these birds remained in California. Then, state and federal authorities took action. They protected nesting grounds and banned DDT. Now, pelicans have made a comeback. Thousands of them breed each year and produce healthy chicks.

The peregrine falcon was once found throughout the United States, as well as in many other parts of the world. Since ancient times, people have used falcons as hunting birds. Falconers carry the birds of prey on their wrists and then release them to kill other birds in midair. The peregrine falcon is the fastest bird in the world. As it dives after its prey, it streaks through the sky at speeds of up to 200 miles an hour (322 km/h)!

Because many of the birds eaten by falcons in the United States contained DDT in their bodies, the chemicals passed into the bodies of the falcons. As a result, they started to lay eggs with shells so thin that few chicks hatched. By 1964, falcons had completely disappeared east of the Mississippi River.

In 1970, scientists at Cornell University, in Ithaca, New York, established an organization called the Peregrine Fund. They began breeding peregrines in captivity and later releasing them into the wild. Now, the group releases hundreds of birds a year.

"There were no peregrines at all in the eastern United States in 1970, and now there are at least 50 breeding pairs," says Phyllis Dague, of the Peregrine Fund. "They're doing well in the West, too. This is one of the most successful conservation efforts of its kind in the world. We're delighted."

In the next chapter, you'll learn about animals that have become endangered because of overhunting—and you'll discover how people are helping them.

Fed by a human hand, a peregrine falcon chick (below) gets a meal of raw meat. Peregrines were among the most endangered of all birds in the United States because of DDT. Captive breeding and the release of young birds have helped increase the number of falcons. This chick's eyes cannot yet focus, so it does not see the person feeding it. It will not learn to depend on humans for food. When it is about four weeks old, volunteers will take the bird to a release site in the wild.

FRANS LANTING

Out on their own, these young peregrines (right) have been released in the wilds of Minnesota. A paint mark on one wing of each bird—visible on the bird at right—helps scientists identify captive-bred birds. Before their release, the peregrines were kept in nest boxes at the release site. Volunteers brought food for them until they learned to hunt and catch prey. Peregrines prefer high places for building their nests, especially cliffsides—or city skyscrapers. In earlier times, peregrines sometimes nested on European castles and on Egyptian pyramids. DANIEL J. COX

3

Stopping the Killing

On a peaceful morning, a small herd of elephants wanders over a grassland in Africa. Without warning, a gunshot shatters the silence. More guns fire, and soon all the adult animals are dead.

Although laws protect elephants in most of Africa, outlaw hunters—called poachers—continue to shoot these animals for their ivory tusks. Poachers sell the ivory to traders. Each pair of tusks may bring thousands of dollars. In Asian countries, craftsmen carve the ivory into jewelry and other luxury items. Since the days of the Egyptian pharaohs, many people have considered ivory to be nearly as precious as gold.

Not so very long ago, poachers used spears and arrows to hunt. Sometimes the elephants could fight back. More than once, the strong, intelligent animals turned and charged their attackers. Today, however, poachers kill thousands of elephants each year with automatic rifles and machine guns. The animals have no chance against such weapons.

In spite of laws to stop the illegal trade in ivory, poaching and smuggling continue. Experts say that the killing will cease only when tourists and other people stop buying products made of ivory. Hunting animals

In a park in Namibia, an African elephant uses its trunk to blow dust over its body. The dust bath will help protect the elephant's skin from the sun and from the bites of insects. Today, elephants are rapidly disappearing because of poaching—illegal hunting. Some of Africa's parks have lost 90 percent of their elephants in the last ten years. The poachers kill the animals for their ivory tusks, used to make art objects and jewelry.

JIM BRANDENBURG

for profit is the second greatest cause, after loss of habitat, of animal extinctions in the world today.

Throughout history, people have hunted wild animals for food and for sport, as well as for hides or other body parts. One Englishman known as Lord Ripon shot *half a million* birds and mammals before he died at age 71. In Africa and other countries in the 19th century, hunting big game was a popular sport among wealthy Europeans.

On the North American continent, a great slaughter of bison, or American buffalo, took place in the late 1800s. These animals then numbered between 30 and 60 million. They roamed the plains in herds that stretched for miles. As people moved west, they killed millions of bison for their hides—and for fun. Railroad passengers, for example, often shot bison from trains. By 1894, fewer than 50 bison remained in the wild in the United

Startled, a white-tailed deer bounds through a stream (left) in British Columbia, in Canada. For centuries, hunters in North America killed white-tailed deer for meat, hides, and trophies. By 1900, they were in danger of dying out. Laws to limit hunting have helped the deer multiply. Now, they are plentiful.

THOMAS KITCHIN (LEFT)

DOUG PLUMMER

On the National Bison Range, in Montana, a horseman herds bison (above). These beasts once roamed the plains in huge herds, but overhunting nearly wiped them out. By the 1890s, only a few hundred remained in public areas and on private ranches in the United States. Today, there are more than 89,000 in the U. S. and in Canada.

A mother grizzly nurses her cubs at the McNeil River, a sanctuary for grizzly bears in Alaska. Many of the animals come here each summer to feed on the plentiful salmon. People who wish to see the grizzlies must obtain permits and enter the sanctuary only with biologists. In the last two centuries, hunters killed most of the grizzlies in the lower 48 states as threats to livestock or for trophies. Grizzlies are unpredictable and sometimes kill humans, but they much prefer to avoid contact with people.

In Nova Scotia, a province of Canada, gray wolves stand in blowing snow. They live at a research facility where scientists study wolf behavior. Through understanding, people will be able to better protect wolves. In the 1800s, ranchers killed so many of these animals that they nearly disappeared in the United States. Today, most gray wolves live in northern Canada and in Alaska.

States. Eventually laws were passed to protect the wild bison. Without the laws, this symbol of the American West, which later appeared on the U. S. nickel, might now be extinct in the wild.

Once the bison herds were gone, settlers brought in cattle and sheep to graze on the plains. The grizzly bear and the wolf were two predators that had hunted the bison. Now, with that food source gone, they began to prey on cattle and sheep. As a result, humans made an all-out effort to destroy the grizzlies and the wolves.

By 1900, ranchers had shot, poisoned, or trapped thousands of these animals. Today, even though laws protect them, fewer than 900 grizzlies live in the lower 48 states, most in national forests or parks in Wyoming, Montana, and Idaho. About 1,200 wolves live in parts of Minnesota. Montana, Idaho, Wisconsin, and Michigan have a few wolves—fewer than two dozen each.

Another reason people have killed grizzlies, wolves,

and other animals is for their fur and other body parts. Not long ago, American alligators were endangered because so many had been killed for their hides. With protection, they made a successful comeback. Now they are pests in some areas because they are so numerous.

Related reptiles called caimans live in South America. Skin from their bellies and sides is used to make high-fashion shoes, handbags, wallets, watchbands, and belts. A single handbag made of caiman skin may sell for between $1,500 and $3,000.

Brazil protects its caimans by law. Nevertheless, poachers are active. They risk being arrested because of high profits. They enter the marshes by night in canoes, searching for their prey with flashlights. When they spot a caiman's eyes above the water, they shoot to kill.

A turtle rests on the head of a caiman (left), a relative of the alligator, in a swamp in South America. Eyes of many other turtles peer from the surrounding water. Although they look quite fierce, caimans eat mostly fish and snails. Hunters kill these animals for their skins, used to make shoes, handbags, and other items.

BRIAN ROGERS/BIOFOTOS (LEFT)

RANDALL HYMAN

In the South American country of Brazil, Asturio Ferreira dos Santos, former director of the state game commission, displays caiman skins seized from poachers. A million caimans are killed illegally every year. High profits tempt the poachers. In one night, a poacher may take a hundred caimans, earning $3 to $5 a skin.

53

Why do people buy products that come from the bodies of endangered or protected species? "Most don't realize that the animals are being illegally killed," says Lynne Hardie, of TRAFFIC, the branch of the World Wildlife Fund that keeps track of trade in wildlife products. "We use magazine ads and exhibits at airports to encourage the public to stop buying such products."

Because they have been overhunted, some species of rhinoceros are among the most endangered animals in the world. These animals, which live in Africa and Asia, remind many people of dinosaurs. A rhinoceros has tough armorlike hide and one or two large pointed horns on its snout. The horns are made not of bone, but of keratin, a substance found as the hard tips of the rhino's toes and in your hair and fingernails. The horns are sometimes used as weapons of defense. Strangely, though, these horns have cost thousands of rhinos their lives and may even cause the extinction of some species of these animals.

For thousands of years, many people in Asia have believed that rhino horn has magical powers. Medicines made from ground rhino horn, these people feel, can cure such ailments as fevers, toothaches, epilepsy, and even insanity. In addition, men in the Middle Eastern country of Yemen greatly value daggers with handles carved from rhino horn. Thousands are sold every year for as much as $11,000 *each*.

Because of high profits, poachers who hunt rhinos may not hesitate to shoot park rangers who get in their way. Guarding rhinos and elephants in African parks is both difficult and dangerous. "One problem is that many of the parks are so large," says Rick Weyerhaeuser, director of the World Wildlife Fund's Africa Program. "Several of the parks are as big as Connecticut and have only a few hundred rangers." Conservation groups are helping by sending vehicles and equipment

A black rhinoceros munches grass amid cattle egrets in Africa's Serengeti National Park, in Tanzania. Poachers have killed nearly all the rhinos in this park. The black rhino is still the most abundant species of rhino, but it is disappearing faster than any other. Many Asian people believe that rhino horn has magical powers to prevent aging and to cure ailments. Scientific tests show, however, that the horns have no medicinal value. Today, a single rhino horn may sell for more than $10,000.

MITSUAKI IWAGO

for patrolling the parks. The African nation of Kenya has put electrified fences around sections of its parks to protect rhinoceroses. The fences discourage poachers and give the animals a safer place to mate and to raise their young.

Perhaps the most important protection for rhinos and other endangered wildlife is international law. In 1975, several nations signed a treaty called the Convention on International Trade in Endangered Species of Wild Fauna and Flora (CITES). The treaty lists species of endangered animals and plants. All of the signing nations agree to protect these species by regulating their import or export. Violators of CITES regulations may be fined or even sent to prison. Close to a hundred nations have now signed the treaty.

Ann Haas works for the Division of Law Enforcement of the U. S. Fish and Wildlife Service, which helps enforce CITES regulations. All shipments are subject

KEVIN SCHAFER

ROBERT CAPUTO

It is illegal to sell these imported shoes, purses, and key chains (left) in the United States. All were made from the skins of endangered reptiles. Under an international treaty to protect wildlife, such goods may not be brought into the United States. Smugglers who break the law may pay fines of up to $20,000 and may even go to prison.

Watching for poachers, an armed ranger guards white rhinos in Meru National Park, in Kenya. As prices for rhino horn go up, poaching increases. Sometimes, rangers are shot to death while defending the lives of the animals. Kenya and other African nations need more guards and patrol vehicles to protect the remaining rhinos.

At the San Diego Zoo, in California, zoo educator Sheri Augst teaches students about endangered species. She shows things like a tiger claw charm or a giraffe tail bracelet. Then the students visit the animals that people kill for valuable parts. Many zoos do more than exhibit animals. They encourage people to help save species.

JAMES BALOG (BOTH)

to official inspection when coming into the U. S. or leaving it. "Smugglers of wildlife often fake import or export permits," says Haas. "They also try to hide animals in false-bottomed boxes. Wildlife trade is big business. The service seizes millions of dollars' worth of animals and products every year."

Another way people are helping wildlife is through educational programs in zoos. For example, Sheri Augst, of the San Diego Zoo, in California, introduces students to various animals and explains why they are threatened or endangered. The students learn that tigers and leopards are disappearing because some people want their fur for coats. Other people believe the skins and teeth are magic charms against evil spirits. Students also discover that poachers kill giraffes and cut off their tails, which are then used to make bracelets and other items. The pupils find out that nine out of ten birds, such as parrots, smuggled for the live-pet trade die before they reach their destinations.

"Superstition and greed cause many animals to die. I tell the students they can help," says Augst, "by visiting pet stores and making sure that no endangered animals are present. I also tell them which government agency to report violations to." Augst encourages them

Ray Knippenberg, Jr., 9, of Santee, California, meets a desert tortoise called Lightning. "He felt smooth," says Ray. Zoo educators brought Lightning into the classroom and told the students about endangered species. So many desert tortoises have been captured to be kept as pets that they are endangered. Now, laws protect them.

to tell anyone going to foreign countries *not* to buy souvenirs made from wildlife products.

Learn more about how *you* can help save wildlife on page 96, in Chapter 5.

Today, some animals once nearly extinct because of overhunting have made amazing comebacks with human help. A good example is the trumpeter swan. In early colonial days, huge flocks of these great white birds migrated over most of North America. Then, in the mid-1800s, people started hunting swans for their feathers. Some of the feathers decorated ladies' hats. Others became quill pens. The soft underfeathers made warm coverlets. People had killed so many swans by the early 20th century that they were near extinction. Scientists estimate that by the 1930s only about a hundred of these birds remained in the world. Just 69 had survived in the United States.

In 1935, the Red Rock Lakes National Wildlife Refuge, in Montana, became a sanctuary for trumpeters. There, the birds multiplied, and breeding pairs could be sent to other refuges. Now, trumpeter swans have made a real comeback. *(Continued on page 65)*

JEFF FOOTT

ART WOLFE (RIGHT)

Thigh-deep in water, Richard Sjostrom (above) holds a trumpeter swan egg up to the light. A biologist at the Red Rock Lakes National Wildlife Refuge, in Montana, he is checking the undeveloped chick inside. Trumpeter swans have made a comeback since 1930, when overhunting had made them nearly extinct.

An adult trumpeter swan (right) guards its young, called cygnets (SIG-nuts), at the Kenai National Wildlife Refuge, in Alaska. To prevent disturbance of the swans, the refuge prohibits aircraft from landing on lakes where the swans nest. These baby swans, only days old, can already swim. They will stay with their parents for about a year.

Stretching its wings, a male trumpeter swan warns other males to stay away from its breeding territory in Yellowstone National Park, in Wyoming. Largest of all swans, the trumpeter may weigh up to 30 pounds (14 kg) and have a wingspan of up to 8 feet (2 m). The swan gets its name from the call it makes, which some say is similar to the sound of a French horn.

MICHAEL S. QUINTON

(Continued from page 60) Today, there are more than 10,000 of them living in the wild.

Another animal making a comeback is the vicuña (vi-KOON-yuh), of South America. Centuries ago, the Inca Indians sheared the wool of these graceful hoofed animals to make a fine, soft cloth. Only members of royalty were allowed to wear it.

When the Europeans came to South America, they began to kill vicuñas for their wool rather than shear them. Over many years, people continued to kill the animals. By the 1960s, fewer than 8,000 vicuñas remained. By 1969, more effective laws were passed—mained. By 1969, more effective laws were passed—and enforced—to prohibit the killing. Recently, the government of Peru began a program to allow people to shear the animals and to sell the wool. With this protection, the vicuña population has grown to more than 100,000.

By the mid-1960s, the polar bear, too, appeared to be in danger of dying out because of overhunting. People killed it for its fur and for trophies. Scientists from the five nations where polar bears live—Canada, the United States, Norway, Denmark, and the Soviet Union—agreed to cooperate in gathering information that could help save the bears. Using large boats and helicopters, scientists followed polar bears. They tranquilized the animals and put tags on them. Then they attached

ROLAND SEITRE/PITCH (LEFT)

WILLIAM L. FRANKLIN

Vicuñas roam a grassy mountainside (left) in Peru. These South American animals are related to the camel. For years, they were hunted for their wool, which can be woven into a fine, soft cloth. Once near extinction, vicuñas are now protected on government preserves. Although some hunting is allowed, the preferred way to obtain the wool is by shearing.

At a research center in Peru, a herder swings his lasso to rope an animal for shearing (above). The herd is made up of both vicuñas and paco-vicuñas. Paco-vicuñas resulted when scientists bred vicuñas with alpacas. Alpacas are similar animals but have thicker wool and are not endangered. This experiment, of only limited success, was part of the effort to save the vicuña.

collars with radio transmitters to track the bears.

The scientists learned that trophy hunters and fur trappers killed at least a thousand polar bears a year. This information led to an agreement signed by all five of the nations to prohibit polar bear hunting in the Arctic Ocean. Because people native to the area have always hunted polar bears, they may still do so. Now, the bears are no longer considered in danger of extinction.

"It's a real success story, not only for polar bears, but also for international cooperation in helping wildlife," says Dr. Charles Jonkel, one of the biologists who studied the bears in Canada.

Although humans have threatened many species, animals are sometimes responsible for killing off other species of animals. Find out how in Chapter Four.

Biologist Charles Jonkel (below) attaches an ear tag to a tranquilized polar bear on arctic ice in Canada. Dr. Jonkel tagged and tracked many polar bears to help save them. "It can be risky," he says. "Once I approached a big male I thought was asleep — only to find that the tranquilizing dart had not fired! I was lucky to get away unhurt."

Northern giant, the polar bear (right) may grow to 1,600 pounds (726 kg). It spends most of its life hunting seals in the icy Arctic Ocean. By the 1960s, polar bears were rapidly disappearing. Fur trappers and trophy hunters, using snowmobiles and aircraft, tracked down and killed a thousand bears a year. In 1973, five nations agreed to stop the hunting of polar bears except by people native to the area. Now, there are up to 40,000 polar bears.

4 Protecting Native Species

Giant tortoises are among the oldest of earth's creatures. Millions of years ago, even before the days of the dinosaurs, ancestors of these huge tortoises lived on earth. Giant tortoises once were common. Today, they are rare. One of the largest species of these giants is the Galápagos tortoise. It lives on the Galápagos Islands of Ecuador, a country in South America. The islands are located in the Pacific Ocean 600 miles (966 km) west of the mainland.

When Spanish explorers discovered the islands in 1535, they named them after the tortoises, which they found living there in enormous herds. *Galápagos* means "tortoises" in Spanish.

Giant tortoises are calm, plodding creatures that spend most of their time feeding on plants and sleeping. They weigh as much as 600 pounds (272 kg). Some have shells that measure more than 4 feet (1 m) long. These reptiles are some of the longest-lived creatures in the world. Scientists believe they may live more than 100 years, perhaps even more than 150 years. Yet the gentle giants now face possible extinction because of the activities of humans.

The explorers who found the tortoises soon learned

Threatened giant, a Galápagos tortoise slowly emerges from a mud wallow on Isabela Island, one of the Galápagos Islands. Peaceful plant-eaters, these tortoises had no enemies until Europeans arrived in the 1500s. For centuries, people killed the tortoises for their meat and oil. In addition, animals that came with the Europeans ate the eggs and the young of the tortoises — and their food. Today, Galápagos tortoises need human help to survive.

FRANS LANTING

that they were good to eat. For the next 300 years, pirates, traders, whale and seal hunters, and settlers killed hundreds of thousands of tortoises for their meat. For long sea voyages, sailors stored hundreds of them alive, stacked on their backs aboard ship. They could live for more than a year without food or water. Ships' cooks killed them to make a stew called sea pie. Later, when people found that the fat of the tortoises could be made into a useful oil, many more were killed.

Today, laws protect giant tortoises. The Galápagos Islands are now a national park of Ecuador, and harming the tortoises is prohibited. Yet, of the 14 original subspecies of tortoises that lived on different islands, only 11 remain. Some of those 11 have very few survivors. One subspecies has a single remaining individual: a male called Lonesome George.

Now the greatest danger to the tortoises and to other species of native wildlife on the Galápagos comes from animals that people once brought to the islands. Pigs, cats, dogs, black rats, goats, and donkeys roamed freely and multiplied. They ate the tortoises, their eggs, and the plants that the tortoises needed for food. (Find out more about this on pages 72–73.) Descendants of the introduced animals continue to destroy tortoises. Now, there are fewer than 15,000 remaining.

Scientists from all over the world come to the Charles Darwin Research Station to study the wildlife of the Galápagos. One such scientist is Susan Schafer, a herpetologist (HER-puh-TAHL-uh-juhst), or one who specializes in reptiles and amphibians. On the staff of the San Diego Zoo, in California, she has spent time in the Galápagos working to save the giant tortoises.

"To protect the tortoises on some islands," says Schafer, "park wardens collect the eggs and raise the young in captivity." Otherwise, species not native to the Galápagos would eat them. (Continued on page 75)

In a quiet pond on Isabela Island, several tortoises rest and cool off. They can also escape biting insects here. The slow-moving animals spend 16 hours a day sleeping, half submerged in mud or burrowed into thick brush. Perhaps the longest-lived creatures in the world, giant tortoises may survive more than 150 years. Once, there were many, many thousands of these animals. Today, fewer than 15,000 remain.

FRANS LANTING

Dangerous New Arrivals

On many voyages during the 1800s, explorers, pirates, traders, and whale and seal hunters visited remote islands to rest, to explore, or to search for food. When they went ashore, they took along various kinds of domestic animals. Often, these animals proved harmful to native wildlife. Here, you can see the problems that developed on the Galápagos Islands, off the coast of South America.

First, a ship anchored near one of the islands (1). Then crewmen in small boats brought ashore various supplies and animals. They brought donkeys as pack animals, pigs and goats as sources of food, and dogs and cats as pets and "mousers." Black rats had been unwelcome passengers on the ship. Those that had escaped the cats' claws somehow managed to reach land.

Once ashore, the domestic animals were turned loose to take care of themselves. The dogs found reptiles called marine iguanas (2) and promptly ate them. The rats and cats discovered that newly hatched tortoises made tasty meals (3,4).*

Meanwhile, the hungry goats and donkeys gobbled up grasses and other plants (5,6) that the native tortoises needed for food. The pigs discovered that the eggs of ground-nesting birds, such as petrels, as well as the birds themselves (7), were good to eat. The pigs raided tortoise nests, too.

Even in ponds on island hilltops (8), the giant tortoises were not safe. Humans—the most dangerous enemies of all—captured them and carried them aboard ship (9). Sailors kept them as food for the voyage home.

In time, non-native species ran wild over the islands. Even today, they continue to threaten native plants and animals. Many of the animals, such as the tortoises, are severely endangered and need protection to survive.

*The tortoise eggs in this painting are exposed for viewing. Normally, they are buried about 1 foot (30 cm) underground.

LOIS SLOAN

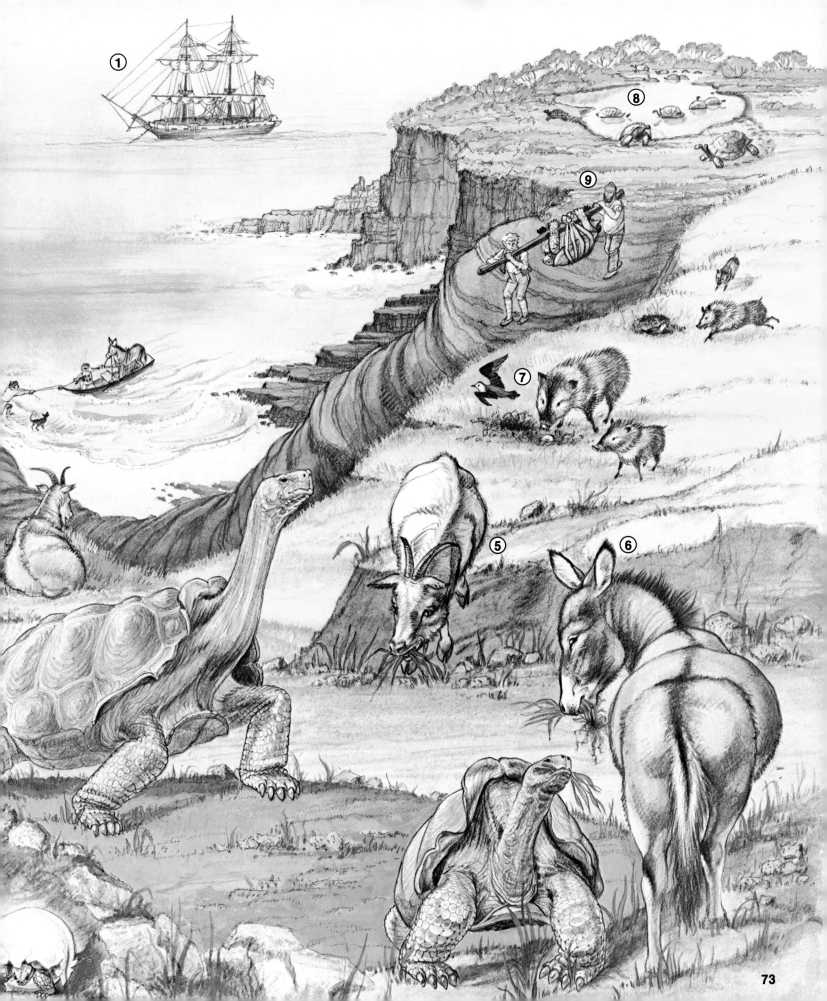

JIM BRANDENBURG

(Continued from page 70)   The wardens find the nests and take the eggs to the research station. There, they hatch in sun-heated incubators. Afterward, the baby tortoises stay in a rat-proof enclosure until they are no longer in danger of being eaten—sometimes until they are ten years old. Then the wardens release them.

"Before setting a tortoise free, wardens paint a small number on the shell. The number identifies it as a captive-raised animal," Schafer explains. "When wardens find a wild tortoise, they cut a small notch on the edge of its shell. This enables researchers to keep count of how many tortoises there are."

So far, more than 900 captive-raised tortoises are alive. They are doing well in the Galápagos, thanks to the help of concerned scientists and park staff.

The Galápagos Islands are only one example of a worldwide problem. As people have traveled all over the globe, they have taken plants and animals with them from place to place. These non-native species often spread out of control, causing serious problems for native wildlife.

In 1851, European settlers brought red deer to New Zealand, an island nation in the Pacific Ocean, southeast of Australia. The settlers wanted to have a large animal for sport hunting. The red deer had no enemies in their new home, so they multiplied rapidly. Large numbers of them stripped the land of grass and shrubs, destroying the food supply of native animals.

More than a hundred years later, farmers decided to domesticate the deer. Farmers now capture the animals with nets shot from helicopters. Then they manage them in herds much like domestic cows. Deer antlers are sold for medicinal purposes. The meat is sold for food. Today, deer farming is a successful business, and red deer no longer threaten New Zealand's wildlife.

Rabbits brought to Australia also became a problem.

Hovering low over a mountain slope in New Zealand, a man in a helicopter captures a wild red deer in a net. The weighted net, fired from a net gun, traps the deer. Brought from England in the 1800s, red deer multiplied rapidly. They stripped the land of plants, leaving little food for native wildlife. To control the deer, farmers have begun to raise them like cattle. Their antlers are sold for medicinal purposes, and their meat is sold for food.

75

A ring-tailed rock wallaby (left) watches for predators in southern Australia. Members of the kangaroo family, wallabies feed mostly on grasses that were once plentiful in their habitat. Today the ring-tailed rock wallaby is an endangered species, primarily because non-native rabbits and goats have destroyed so many plants.

JOHN CANCALOSI (BOTH)

In South Australia, Dr. John Wamsley (above) inspects an electrified fence around a sanctuary he established for native wildlife. The 35 acres are now home to thousands of plants and animals. The fence keeps out rabbits, goats, foxes, and other non-native animals that are harmful to the native species. Private fencing projects may help save endangered Australian creatures.

In 1859, a wealthy Englishman living there decided that he would like to amuse himself with rabbit hunting. He ordered two dozen of the animals to be shipped from England, thinking that they and their offspring would be plenty to provide him with sport.

In Australia, the rabbits had few predators, such as foxes, which had kept them under control in England. Within a few years, those two dozen rabbits had multiplied to thousands. Eventually, there were billions of them. They ate many kinds of plants, destroying the habitats of native wildlife and vast areas of farmland.

For years, people tried to get rid of the rabbits. They even imported English foxes as predators. The foxes caused *another* problem. They preyed not only on the rabbits but also on small animals native to the country.

Eventually, a virus killed many of the rabbits. Although it has not wiped out the hardy animals, the virus keeps them somewhat under control. Rabbits are still pests on this island continent. They, along with the goats, cattle, and sheep brought by settlers, have destroyed much of the plant life needed as food by Australian animals, such as bettongs and rock wallabies. Both of these small kinds of kangaroos are dying out because they lack food and because foxes prey on them.

D r. John Wamsley, a former mathematics professor, grew concerned about the problems of native Australian wildlife. In 1982, he established a sanctuary for both plants and animals. Called the Warrawong Sanctuary, it covers 35 acres and has an electrified fence to keep out rabbits, foxes, and other non-native species. While getting rid of non-native plants and animals inside the sanctuary, Wamsley planted thousands of native trees, shrubs, and grasses. Then he brought in native animals. Warrawong Sanctuary now provides a habitat where endangered Australian species can live in safety.

On Lord Howe Island, east of the Australian mainland, the flightless wood hen was nearly extinct by the late 1970s. Again, the problem had been caused by pigs, cats, and rats brought to the island nearly 200 years earlier. Descendants of those animals ate the defenseless wood hens and their eggs faster than the birds could reproduce.

To save the Lord Howe Island wood hens, which had been reduced to about 20 birds, biologists killed most of the non-native predators. They also captured three pairs of the birds and allowed them to breed. The scientists later set the captive-bred birds free in their native habitat, where they multiplied.

Non-native animals also have caused great problems

in North America. Two of the most destructive immigrants have been the house sparrow—sometimes called the English sparrow—and the starling. Well-meaning admirers brought these two species to the United States from Europe in the 1800s.

The birds quickly became a problem. They multiplied, spread rapidly, and began driving away native songbirds. One of the species most severely affected is the eastern bluebird. With royal blue back feathers and rosy breast, it was once almost as common as the robin. It nests only in cavities, such as old tree hollows, in open country. Since sparrows and starlings also nest in cavities, they drive out the gentle bluebirds, often breaking their eggs or killing their babies. In this century, the eastern bluebird population may have

Small and flightless, the Lord Howe Island wood hen (below) is one of the world's rarest birds. Sailors visiting the island ate them. Non-native pigs, cats, and rats ate not only the birds but also their eggs and their food. By the 1970s, only 20 wood hens remained. Scientists saved the species by breeding a few pairs in captivity while ridding the island of most predators. Now captive-bred birds are making a comeback in their native habitat.

Lord Howe Island (right), located off the east coast of Australia, appears to be unspoiled. Yet, like many isolated islands, it suffered loss of its wildlife when humans came ashore and brought animals with them. Discovered by the British in 1788, the island was soon overrun with cats, rats, pigs, and goats. These animals killed off many species of native birds.

Home, sweet home! A female eastern bluebird perches on a nest box. Her mate has brought an insect to feed the babies inside. During this century, the number of bluebirds decreased. House sparrows and starlings, two kinds of birds imported from Europe, were largely responsible. They took over the bluebirds' nesting sites. Without places to raise their young, bluebirds became fewer and fewer. Now, thousands of people have come to the rescue by building nest boxes and monitoring them.

dropped by as much as 90 percent. Today, however, it appears to be making a comeback, thanks in part to the work of the North American Bluebird Society. Dr. Lawrence Zeleny founded the society in 1978. After retiring from his job, he began to devote his life to helping the bluebird. He put up about 60 nest boxes near his home in Maryland. Soon, bluebirds moved in. Now from 100 to 200 or more young are raised in the boxes every year.

The Bluebird Society urges people across the continent to put up nest boxes. Today, the Society has more than 5,000 members. They have put up thousands of boxes in the United States and in Canada.

The nest boxes are simple to build. They have small holes that starlings cannot squeeze through. House sparrows *can* get into the boxes, so a human must check them often during the nesting season to make sure sparrows do not move in.

"Sometimes saving wildlife seems like too big a job for one individual to make a difference," says Zeleny. "But helping bluebirds is different. *Anyone* can do it, and each person's help is important."

According to Zeleny, the bluebird population has dramatically increased wherever people have set out enough nest boxes in suitable habitats and cared for them properly. Bluebirds are still in serious trouble, however. "Without the help of many more people, bluebirds are in danger of disappearing within the next 50 to 100 years," he cautions. "If enough people help, however, I think we can save them."

Would *you* like to help the bluebird make a comeback near you? Write for information and instructions for building a nest box to the North American Bluebird Society, Box 6295, Silver Spring, Maryland 20906-0295.

In the next chapter, you'll explore some of the latest scientific techniques for helping wildlife. You'll also find out more ways that you can help.

Opening wide for dinner, baby bluebirds eight days old get a meal from their father. Young bluebirds usually leave the nest after 18 days. The parent birds built this nest in a hollow log in the photographer's backyard. He had fitted the log with a removable top for taking pictures. Since colonial times, bluebirds have been symbols of hope and happiness. Now, with the help of human friends, these native birds are making a welcome comeback.

5 Safeguarding the Future

"Baby gorillas are playful and cute," says Sue Doleshal, a keeper of gorillas at the San Diego Wild Animal Park, in California. "And gorilla mothers are very warm and affectionate. When the babies get scared, their mothers hold and cuddle them just as human mothers do with their babies."

Full-grown male gorillas weigh more than 400 pounds (181 kg). Although large, gorillas are shy and peaceful. Mainly vegetarians, they eat fruits and other plant foods.

At the Wild Animal Park, which covers hundreds of acres, lowland gorillas live together in a large family group. Their home at the park is a grassy hillside with rocks and tree stumps to climb on, a pool to cool off in, and cavelike doorways that lead to private rooms, where the animals can go when they want to be away from people.

Visitors to the park enjoy watching the gorillas behave naturally—much as they would in the wild in west-central Africa. The natural setting helps the gorillas mate and have young more easily.

This is important today, because both the lowland

Time for a hug! Schroeder, a baby lowland gorilla, one year old, snuggles in the arms of his "aunt" Vila at the San Diego Wild Animal Park, in California. In their native west-central Africa, the gorillas are dying out because of poaching and habitat loss. Poachers kill the adults and take the babies to sell for high prices. Zoos are working to save gorillas by helping them breed in captivity and by refusing to buy wild gorillas caught by poachers.

JAMES BALOG

gorilla and the mountain gorilla are severely endangered in the wild. People have destroyed their habitats and killed many of the animals. Poachers kill the adults and capture the babies. Then they sell them to animal dealers. Few wild gorillas are left. Without human help, they might die out.

Zoos around the world are trying to encourage endangered animals to breed in captivity. In some cases, such breeding is difficult.

"Gorillas are hard to breed because they are choosy about their mates," says Doleshal. "They need plenty of space, and they need to live in groups. Young female

gorillas learn to be mothers by watching older ones."

Seven baby gorillas have been born at the Wild Animal Park since 1973. One reason for this success is that humans have learned more about caring for captive animals. Another reason is that zoos are cooperating by exchanging and lending animals for breeding. Today, zoos often are no longer just showcases for animals. Many of them are saving wildlife for the future.

Some animals, in fact, exist only in zoos. One is Przewalski's (per-zhih-VAHL-skeez) horse. It is the world's only true wild horse. No one has seen it in the wild since 1968. It once roamed in China, Mongolia, and the Soviet Union. Humans overhunted the wild horses, and cattle took over their grazing areas. The

Chinese alligators, like this hatchling at the Bronx Zoo (above), may one day live only in captivity. In their native China, they have nearly disappeared. People have killed them, and the expanding human population has changed their marsh and river habitats. Only about 500 of this species remain in the wild. After years of study, experts now know how to help the alligators breed in zoos.

Przewalski's horses (above) make themselves at home in the Bronx Zoo, in New York City. This species has disappeared from its habitat in central Asia. Zoos have helped Przewalski's horses survive and multiply. In the next few years, some will be placed in their wild habitat. On protected ranges, the species will run free once again.

A Bali mynah (right) perches on a twig at the National Zoo's breeding farm in Virginia. Native to the Asian country of Indonesia, Bali mynahs have been hunted almost to extinction. Zoo breeding has been a vital factor in saving the species. Now a plan exists to place some of the birds in a protected part of their habitat.

herds gradually shrank until only 13 horses survived.

Today, more than 600 Przewalski's horses live in zoos. All are descendants of the 13 survivors. Many nations working together have participated in saving the species from extinction.

"Now," says Dr. Oliver Ryder, a researcher at the San Diego Zoo, "the animals are multiplying well. It is time to put some of them back in the wild."

According to Ryder, some Przewalski's horses will be released during the next several years. Eventually, they will live as free-ranging herds on the plains of China, Mongolia, and the Soviet Union.

"The horses will be placed in their original habitat gradually," Ryder explains, "in very large fenced areas. If they do well, the fences will be taken down. It's very exciting that we can do this."

The golden lion tamarin is a tiny reddish gold monkey that once lived throughout the Atlantic coastal forest in Brazil. Today, only 2 percent of its habitat is left. People have chopped down the trees. They have caught the beautiful monkeys to sell as pets. Now, only about 400 tamarins remain in the wild.

Like a bright flame among green leaves, a golden lion tamarin darts through trees in the Poço das Antas Biological Reserve, in Brazil. Golden lion tamarins nearly died out from loss of habitat and from being hunted for the pet trade. In 1984, scientists of the National Zoo, in Washington, D. C., began releasing zoo-bred tamarins in the wild. By tracking the animals with radio equipment, the experts learned that many of them survived and successfully bred with their wild relatives.

Graceful antelope called Arabian oryx climb on rocks in the San Diego Wild Animal Park, in California. Native to deserts of the Middle East, Arabian oryx were nearly killed off by sports hunters. Conservationists took the eight remaining animals to the Phoenix Zoo, in Arizona, and to the San Diego Wild Animal Park. Now, enough Arabian oryx have been born in captivity to send more than 35 to Middle Eastern preserves.

Zoos all over the world are working together to raise these monkeys in captivity. In 1984, scientists at the National Zoo, in Washington, D. C., began a project to release zoo-bred tamarins into a protected part of their Brazilian habitat. Would these captive-raised tamarins be able to survive in the jungle?

"It would be just as if *you* were suddenly dropped into a rain forest for the first time," says Dr. James Dietz, a biologist working on this project. "You would be frightened and hungry. So would zoo-bred monkeys. You wouldn't know how to find your way around in the maze of branches. Neither would the tamarins."

To help the monkeys survive, scientists spent weeks in Brazil training them to find food and to move around in large cages in the forest. The zoo-bred animals were accustomed to being served two large meals at regular times every day. In the forest, they would have to find their own food. To train them, the scientists hid food under tree leaves or in cracks. They taught the tamarins to catch insects. They also gave the tamarins practice in climbing among tangled branches and vines.

Finally, it was time to open the cages. Timidly at first, the tamarins ventured out. Many of them gradually learned to live in the forest. Some mated with wild tamarins and had babies. So far, 24 tamarins have been set free, and more will be released soon. At the same time, American and Brazilian scientists have been teaching the local people about saving the forest.

"I'm proud of our work," says Dietz. "Without help, these animals might have become extinct in the wild."

Today, scientists are using advanced techniques to help save endangered species. For example, biologist Dan Wharton, of the Bronx Zoo, in New York City,

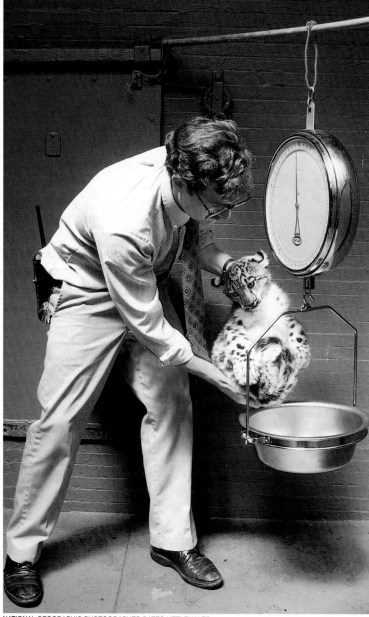

A zoo curator weighs a six-week-old snow leopard cub (above) born at the Bronx Zoo. Officials weigh the young animals regularly to see if they are growing normally. Some cubs born at this zoo are sent to other zoos for breeding. In the last 20 years, zoos have learned a great deal about helping snow leopards breed successfully in captivity.

At the Bronx Zoo, Dan Wharton uses a computer (below) to help the snow leopard. Part of his job is to keep track of all the snow leopards in North American zoos by sex, age, and ancestry. With that information, Wharton can recommend to each zoo how its snow leopards should be bred to produce a population of healthy captive animals. If snow leopards in the wild should ever die out, those in captivity could save the species from extinction.

An adult female snow leopard named Shere prowls through a large new space at the Bronx Zoo (right). In the wild, snow leopards live in the high mountains of India, China, Nepal, and Mongolia. They have become endangered because some people kill them to protect livestock. Others kill them for their fur, which is used to make expensive coats.

coordinates the Snow Leopard Species Survival Plan. He keeps a record of the sex, the age, and the ancestors of all snow leopards in North American zoos. He can recommend which animals should be bred to each other to produce a healthy captive population.

"Thriving zoo-bred snow leopards," says Wharton, "provide an 'insurance policy' against extinction."

Snow leopards are endangered today because of habitat loss and hunting. If they should die out in the wild, captive animals could be released into preserves, thanks to the work of zoos.

To help some species multiply as rapidly as possible, scientists use a procedure called embryo transplant. Dr. Betsy Dresser, of the Cincinnati Zoo, for example, takes embryos—tiny developing animals—from their mothers' bodies. Then she puts the embryos into the bodies

That's no ordinary calf peering over the neck of its "mother" (left). It is a gaur, a species of wild cattle highly endangered in its native Asia. The "mother" is a Holstein cow. The calf was born at the Bronx Zoo after an embryo transplant. To perform such a transplant, scientists gently take a tiny developing baby, called an embryo, from the body of its real mother. Then they put it into the body of a female whose species may not be endangered. This method helps endangered species multiply more rapidly.

Rusty spotted cats like this one (above) in the Cincinnati Zoo, in Ohio, live in Sri Lanka, an island south of India. They may soon disappear in the wild. Using the 16 captive ones now in zoos, scientists are working to increase their numbers. Embryos from rusty spotted cats will be placed in the bodies of domestic cats. The substitute "mom cats" will help the real moms by bearing and raising many rusty spotted kittens.

Dr. Betsy Dresser, a scientist at the Cincinnati Zoo, is creating a "frozen zoo" (right). Each of the plastic straws she holds contains an embryo taken from its mother's body. She is putting the straws into a container of nitrogen, a gas that becomes a liquid at very low temperatures. Cooled to -196° Celsius (-385°F), the nitrogen instantly freezes the embryos and keeps them safe for later use. The container can hold a thousand straws, so it is called a frozen zoo. If any of the species in the frozen zoo becomes extinct in the wild, the embryos may be thawed and used to produce new individuals.

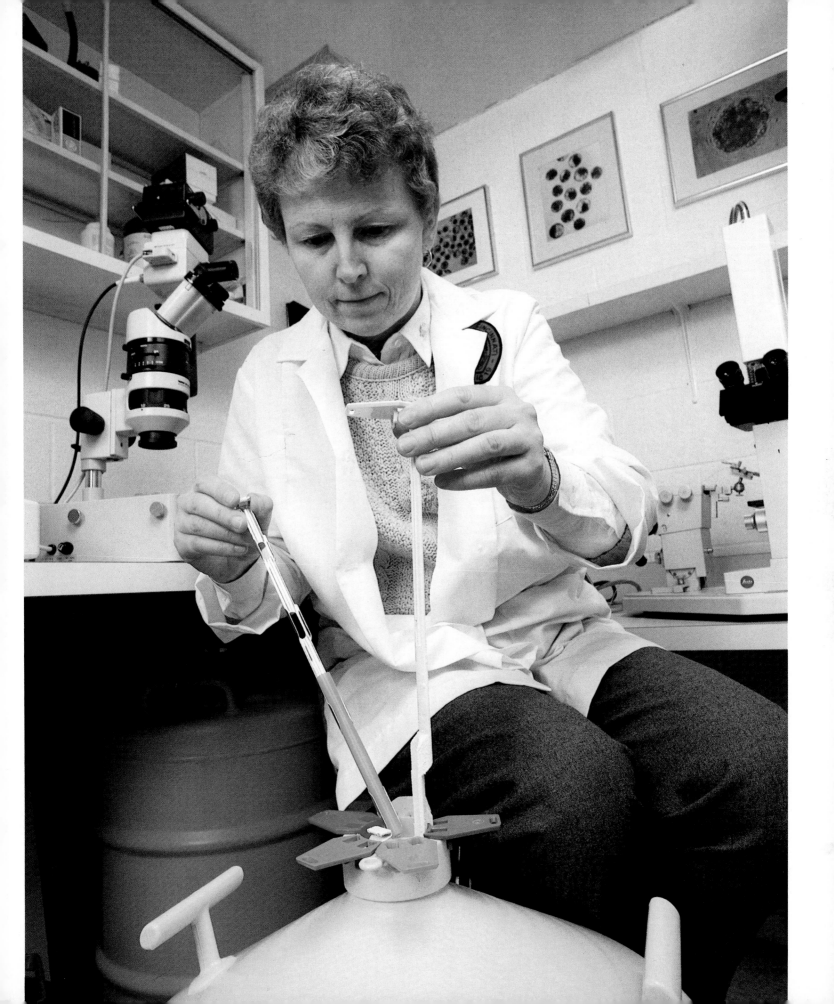

of similar animals whose species are not endangered. After the embryos fully develop, the substitute mother gives birth to young of the endangered species.

"If a species is very low in numbers, embryo transfer helps it reproduce quickly," says Dresser. "We can transfer as many as 70 embryos at a time from an endangered cat to other females to produce young."

Another new technique that Dresser, among other scientists, uses involves freezing the embryos of endangered species. In the future, the embryos may be thawed and used to produce healthy babies.

"Many species are becoming extinct before we can help them," says Dresser. "Now 'frozen zoos' may prevent extinctions from occurring."

A species rapidly nearing extinction in 1941 was the

Flying low, a whooping crane (left) heads toward its winter home in the Aransas National Wildlife Refuge, on the coast of Texas. Tallest of all North American birds, whooping cranes grow to be 5 feet (152 cm) in height. They nearly died out from loss of marshes and from overhunting. Today, they are slowly making a comeback.

ENTHEOS (LEFT)

THOMAS D. MANGELSEN

A young whooping crane stands next to its foster parents — sandhill cranes — at the Patuxent Wildlife Research Center, in Maryland. Whooping cranes lay two eggs, but raise just one chick. To help produce more of these birds, scientists began taking the extra eggs and placing them in the nests of sandhill cranes. The sandhills raise the chicks as their own. Whooping cranes have increased from 21 birds in 1941 to almost 200 today.

whooping crane. Only 21 of the birds were left. Named for their loud call, whoopers once ranged over much of North America. They nearly died out as people hunted them and drained marshlands for farming.

The remaining whoopers lived in refuges in the United States and in Canada. In 1967, scientists at the Patuxent Wildlife Research Center, in Maryland, developed a daring plan to help whooping cranes multiply.

The experts knew that whooper parents produce two eggs but raise only one chick. They decided to take an egg from each nest and hatch it at the research center. They soon discovered that sandhill cranes would act as substitute parents. The sandhills would sit on the whooper eggs and then raise the chicks as their own. The foster parent plan has worked well. Now, there are nearly 200 whooping cranes.

The future of many of earth's wildlife species depends on the understanding and help of humans everywhere. Today, people can learn about wildlife in several ways.

One way is to visit zoos. In the Bronx Zoo, in New York City, for example, visitors of all ages enjoy realistic exhibits. It is easy for them to imagine that they are in actual habitats halfway across the globe. In the exhibit called JungleWorld, people watch hundreds of wild animals in their natural environments. Part of this exhibit is a treetop observation post. Here, people learn how scientists observe wildlife in the field.

On the West Coast, schoolchildren learn firsthand about helping marine mammals—such as seals, sea lions, and dolphins—at the California Marine Mammal Center. The center, just north of San Francisco, rescues marine mammals that are stranded, sick, or injured. Many staff members are volunteers. Visitors watch the animals being treated for injuries, diseases, pollution poisoning, and other problems. After the workers nurse

Uptown safari. Junior high school students from the Bronx, in New York City, explore JungleWorld, an exhibit at the Bronx Zoo. The huge indoor exhibit is designed to look like different kinds of rain forests. Visitors see animals—such as monkeys, panthers, pythons, tropical birds, and insects—in environments that duplicate their natural surroundings. The exhibit includes tropical trees and other plants, waterfalls, pools, and artificial rock cliffs. Machines create warm temperatures and high humidity.

the animals back to health, they take them to the ocean and let them go.

"There's no more wonderful sight than an animal set free after it's been sick or dying," says Mary Jane Schramm, the center's volunteer public relations director. "That's our reward."

Would *you* like to give wildlife a helping hand? There are many ways you can. Here are some of the things you can do, no matter where you live.

1. *Support conservation organizations that help wildlife.* With your friends and classmates, sponsor a car wash, a bake sale, or other money-making activities.

Then donate the money to help an endangered animal. Write to the World Wildlife Fund* or other conservation groups for information on how you can contribute to a program for endangered animals. Or request that your donation help purchase a jeep, truck, or other vehicle to guard wildlife in African game parks.

2. *Write letters to help wildlife.* You can write to your representatives in state and federal government, urging them to support laws that help endangered species.

3. *Never buy wild animals as pets.* Be sure any pet you buy has been properly raised in captivity and is not a member of an endangered species. Write to TRAFFIC (U.S.A.),* and ask for their free "Buyer Beware" booklet.

4. *Never buy products made from wildlife parts,* such as ivory or reptile-skin items. Write to the Office of Endangered Species* for brochures on how to recognize and avoid such products.

5. *If you travel to a foreign country,* be sure not to harm any local wildlife or buy souvenirs made from their products. Talk with others going abroad and tell them how to protect wildlife.

6. *Find out what laws have been passed* to protect your favorite endangered animal. Write to the Defenders of Wildlife* to find out how people are helping preserve and maintain homes for wildlife. Ask about ways you can help save endangered species.

7. *Volunteer* to help clean up at a wildlife refuge or a zoo, or to do other work there. You can also apply to be a junior zoo keeper.

8. *If you live near an ocean or visit one,* help wildlife there by removing trash from the water. Plastic six-pack holders and pieces of fishing net are especially dangerous. Birds and mammals often become entangled in them.

9. *Help birds by building bird feeders.* Birds often have a hard time finding food in winter. To learn about birds and other kinds of wildlife, write to the National Audubon Society.*

* For the addresses of organizations, see page 103.

Working gently, volunteers at the California Marine Mammal Center, near San Francisco, use a net to lift an orphaned elephant seal from a holding pool. At the center, experts and volunteers work to rescue many marine mammals, including seals, sea lions, dolphins, and whales, that have been stranded and are sick or hurt. The goal is to help the animals recover, and then to release them into the wild.

AL GIDDINGS/OCEAN IMAGES, INC. (BOTH)

Release time! This is the moment everyone enjoys most (right). For the volunteers, it is their reward for a labor of love. As release-team members open cage doors, harbor seals wriggle out and scoot into the sea. Not long ago, little could be done to help most beached animals. Since 1975, however, the California Marine Mammal Center has rescued hundreds of marine mammals stranded on coasts from Oregon to California.

Once the earth was rich with an abundance of wild-life. Today, many species have disappeared because of the activities of humans. Human beings have learned, however, that sometimes they can help vanishing species. California gray whales have come back. Bald eagles are also returning. So are mountain lions, golden lion tamarins, and bluebirds. These animals are living proof that people can save species if they work together.

Our world is the only place in the universe known to have life—and it is incredibly varied, complex, and beautiful. As humans increase in number and crowd the earth, they need to work harder than ever to preserve other species. Biologists and other experts agree that people must learn to live in harmony with all earth's creatures. Some scientists believe that the earth may be a gigantic living organism, whose existence depends on all its creatures living in balance. People are not masters of nature, but part of it.

American Indians seem to have always been aware of this. In 1855, Chief Sealth, of the Duwamish tribe located in present-day Washington State, wrote to the President of the United States. He knew that his people would lose their land to the new "civilized" Americans, and he was concerned about the fate of the land's wild creatures. Here, in part, is what he wrote:

"Every part of the earth is sacred to my people. Every shining pine needle . . . every humming insect is holy in the memory and experience of my people. . . . All things share the same breath—the beasts, the trees, the man. . . . I have seen a thousand rotting buffalos on the prairies, left by the white man who shot them from a passing train. I am a savage and I do not understand. . . . What is man without the beasts? If all the beasts were gone, man would die from great loneliness of spirit, for whatever happens to the beasts also happens to man. All things are connected."

Herds of large antelope called wildebeests migrate across the Serengeti Plain, in East Africa. The Serengeti is one of a few places on earth where wild animals of many kinds still migrate freely, going wherever there is grass to graze or prey to hunt. Some species are threatened now by human predators, who kill them for fur, ivory, and other body parts. People also pollute the land or crowd animals out of their habitats. Can wildlife species survive for future generations to see, to marvel at, and to enjoy? The future depends on what people do today.

MITSUAKI IWAGO

98

A mother cheetah licks her cub's face. These cheetahs live on the Serengeti Plain. Once this species ranged from southern Africa to India. Today, they live only in certain parts of Africa. Pushed from their habitat by farmers and hunted for their beautiful fur, cheetahs in the wild now number only about 10,000. Many people are working to save cheetahs from extinction. With cooperation and dedication, it can be done.

Index

Bold type refers to illustrations;
regular type refers to text.

Where To Write

California Marine Mammal Center
Marin Headlands, GGNRA
Fort Cronkhite, CA 94965

Defenders of Wildlife
Public Information
1244 Nineteenth St., NW
Washington, DC 20036

Global Tomorrow Coalition
1325 G St., NW
Suite 915
Washington, DC 20005-3112

National Association
for Advancement of Humane
Education
Box 362
East Haddam, CT 06423

National Audubon Society
Information Services
950 Third Avenue
New York, NY 10022

Office of Endangered Species
1000 N. Glebe Rd.
Suite 500
Arlington, VA 22201

TRAFFIC (U.S.A.)
1250 Twenty-fourth St., NW
Suite 500
Washington, DC 20037

World Wildlife Fund
1250 Twenty-fourth St., NW
Washington, DC 20037

Library of Congress CIP Data

Rinard, Judith E.
  Wildlife: making a comeback.
  (Books for world explorers)
  Bibliography: p.
  Includes index.
  Summary: Focuses on previously endangered species that have made comebacks and avoided extinction through world efforts toward wildlife conservation.
    1. Wildlife conservation—Juvenile literature.
  [1. Wildlife conservation. 2. Rare animals] I. Title. II. Series.
  QL83.R56 1987   333.9516   87-22078
  ISBN 0-87044-656-8 (regular edition)
  ISBN 0-87044-661-4 (library edition)

CONSULTANTS

Michael E. Soulé, Ph.D., University of Michigan, *Chief Consultant*
Glenn O. Blough, LL.D., Emeritus Professor of Education, University of Maryland, *Educational Consultant*
Nicholas J. Long, Ph.D., *Consulting Psychologist*
Lynda Bush, Ph.D.; and Barbara J. Wood, M.Ed.; Montgomery County (Maryland) Public Schools, *Reading Consultants*

The Special Publications and School Services Division is grateful to the individuals and organizations cited here, as well as to others named or quoted in the text, for their generous cooperation and assistance during the preparation of *WILDLIFE: MAKING A COMEBACK:*

Sheri Augst, Susan F. Schafer, Ken Young, The Zoological Society of San Diego; Theodore N. Bailey, Kenai National Wildlife Refuge; Peigin Barrett, Mary Jane Schramm, California Marine Mammal Center; John Behler, Donald Bruning, James D. Doherty, Ann Robinson, Dan Wharton, New York Zoological Park; Curtis Bohlen, Victor Bullen, Lynne C. Hardie, Emilie H. Mead, and Rick Weyerhaeuser, World Wildlife Fund; Peter Brazaitis, IUCN Crocodile Specialist Group; John Cancalosi, Vida Nature Series; Murray Clark, Ducks Unlimited Canada; James M. Coe, Charles Fowler, National Oceanic and Atmospheric Administration; Charles Cook, Walt Disney's Discovery Island Zoological Park; Phyllis R. Dague, The Peregrine Fund; Betsy Dresser, Ph.D., Cathy Tompson, Cincinnati Zoo; William L. Franklin, Ph.D., Iowa State University of Science; Tom and Pam Gardner; Franklin Gress, University of California, Davis; Ann Haas, Craig A. Koppie, Jon M. Malcolm, Ronald Nowak, Dorn Whitmore, U. S. Fish and Wildlife Service; Thomas F. Hanscom, Sue Doleshal, Peggy Sexton, San Diego Wild Animal Park; Fred D. Harrington; Maurice G. Hornocker, Ph.D., Wildlife Research Institute; Charles Jonkel; Joan Kittrell, Darci Rivers, USDA Forest Service; Terry McEneaney, Yellowstone National Park; Michael Morgan, National Zoological Park; Nan Muckenhirn; Janet Ross, Miami Metrozoo; Richard A. Sellers; Richard Sjostrom; Michael L. Smith; Lee Sochasky, Atlantic Salmon Federation; Gary J. Strachan, California State Parks; Dale L. Sydenstricker, Pacific SeaFari Tours; Merlin D. Tuttle, Ph.D., Bat Conservation International; Marie E. Uehling, Smithsonian Institution; Noel D. Vietmeyer, National Research Council; Jesse R. White, Florida Manatee Research and Educational Foundation, Inc.; Jim Yoakum, Bureau of Land Management; Fred Zeillemaker.

ADDITIONAL READING

Readers may want to check the National Geographic Index in a school or in a public library for related articles and to refer to the following books. ("A" indicates a book for readers at the adult level.)
Batten, Mary, *The Tropical Forest,* Thomas Y. Crowell Company, 1973. Cadieux, Charles L., *These Are the Endangered,* The Stone Wall Press, Inc., 1982 (A). Ehrlich, Paul R., and Anne H. Ehrlich, *Extinction: The Causes and Consequences of the Disappearance of Species,* Random House, 1981 (A). McClung, Robert M., *Lost Wild Worlds,* William Morrow and Company, 1976 (A). Myers, Norman, ed., *Gaia: An Atlas of Planet Management,* Anchor Press/Doubleday & Company Inc., 1984 (A). Ross, Wilda, *The Rainforest,* Coward, McCann & Geoghegan, Inc. 1977. Ryden, Hope, *America's Bald Eagle,* G. P. Putnam's Sons, 1985. Stermer, Dugald, *Vanishing Creatures,* Lancaster-Miller Publishers, 1981 (A). Stewart, Darryl, *From the Edge of Extinction,* Methuen, Inc., 1978 (A).

WILDLIFE: MAKING A COMEBACK
How Humans Are Helping
By Judith E. Rinard

PUBLISHED BY
THE NATIONAL GEOGRAPHIC SOCIETY
WASHINGTON, D. C.

Gilbert M. Grosvenor, *President and Chairman of the Board*
Melvin M. Payne, Thomas W. McKnew, *Chairmen Emeritus*
Owen R. Anderson, *Executive Vice President*
Robert L. Breeden, *Senior Vice President, Publications and Educational Media*

PREPARED BY THE SPECIAL PUBLICATIONS AND SCHOOL SERVICES DIVISION

Donald J. Crump, *Director*
Philip B. Silcott, *Associate Director*
Bonnie S. Lawrence, *Assistant Director*

BOOKS FOR WORLD EXPLORERS

Pat Robbins, *Editor*
Ralph Gray, *Editor Emeritus*
Ursula Perrin Vosseler, *Art Director*
Margaret McKelway, *Associate Editor*
David P. Johnson, *Illustrations Editor*

STAFF FOR *WILDLIFE: MAKING A COMEBACK*

Martha C. Christian, *Managing Editor*
Glover S. Johns, III, *Picture Editor*
Drayton Hawkins, *Art Director*
Sheila M. Green, *Senior Researcher*
Patricia N. Holland, *Special Projects Editor*
Lois Sloan, *Artist*
Barbara Gibson, *Artist (Gameboard art)*
Joan Hurst, *Editorial Assistant*
Bernadette L. Grigonis, Karen L. O'Brien, *Illustrations Assistants*
Aimée L. Clause, *Art Secretary*

ENGRAVING, PRINTING, AND PRODUCT MANUFACTURE:

Robert W. Messer, *Manager;* George V. White, *Senior Assistant Manager;* Vincent P. Ryan, *Assistant Manager;* David V. Showers, *Production Manager;* Lewis R. Bassford, *Production Project Manager;* Gregory Storer, George J. Zeller, Jr., *Senior Assistant Production Managers;* Mark R. Dunlevy, *Film Archivist;* Timothy H. Ewing, *Production Assistant;* Carol R. Curtis, *Senior Production Staff Assistant.*

STAFF ASSISTANTS: Betsy Ellison, Donna L. Hall, Mary Elizabeth House, Kaylene F. Kahler, Sandra F. Lotterman, Eliza C. Morton, Nancy J. White.

MARKET RESEARCH: Mark W. Brown, Joseph S. Fowler, Carrla L. Holmes, Marla Lewis, Donna R. Schoeller, Marsha Sussman, Lisa A. Tunick, Judy Turnbull.

INDEX: Bryan K. Knedler

Composition for *WILDLIFE: MAKING A COMEBACK* by the Typographic section of National Geographic Production Services, Pre-Press Division. Printed and bound by Holladay-Tyler Printing Corp., Glenn Dale, Md. Film preparation by Catharine Cooke Studio, Inc., New York, N.Y.; Lanman-Progressive Co., Washington, D. C.; and NEC, Inc., Nashville, Tenn. Teacher's Guide printed by McCollum Press, Inc., Rockville, Md.